HOT AND COLD

By

Steffi Cavell-Clarke

©2017
Book Life
King's Lynn
Norfolk PE30 4LS

ISBN: 978-1-78637-189-8

Written by:
Steffi Cavell-Clarke

Edited by:
Charlie Ogden

Designed by:
Evie Wright

A catalogue record for this book
is available from the British Library

PHOTO CREDITS

CONTENTS

Words that look like this can be found in the glossary on page 24.

What Is SCIENCE?

What is temperature?

How do we measure temperature?

What is ice made of?

Science can help us to answer many difficult questions. It can also help us to understand the world around us.

What Is TEMPERATURE?

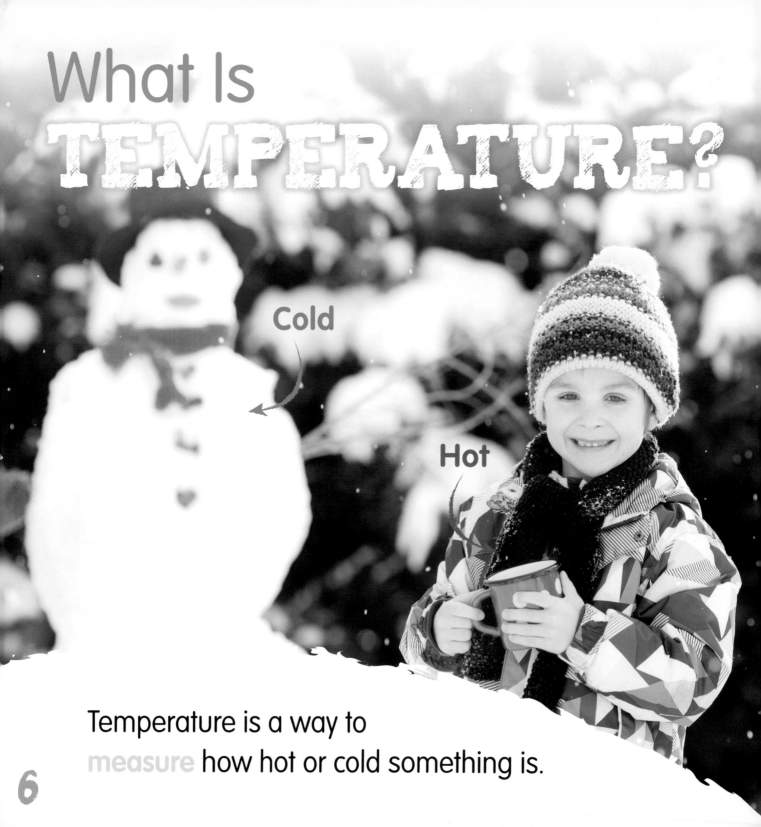

Cold

Hot

Temperature is a way to measure how hot or cold something is.

Some things have a high temperature, like a hot cup of tea. Some things have a low temperature, like an ice cream.

Ice Cream

Cup of Tea

What Is a
THERMOMETER?

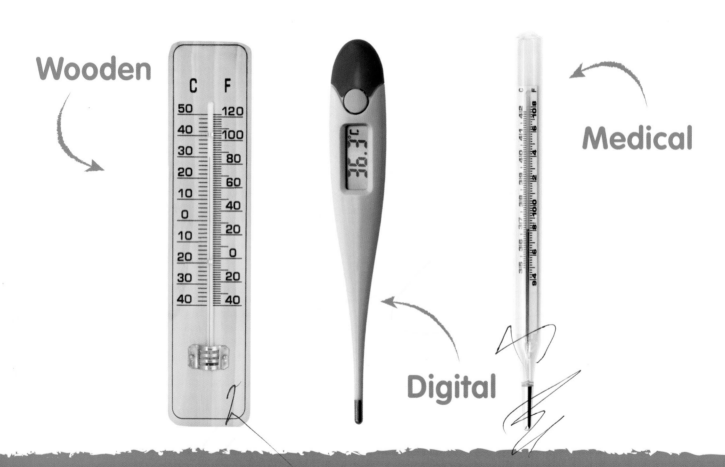

Wooden

Medical

Digital

A thermometer measures temperature. Thermometers can come in many different shapes and sizes.

Temperature is measured in degrees. It can be measured in Celsius (°C) or in Fahrenheit (°F).

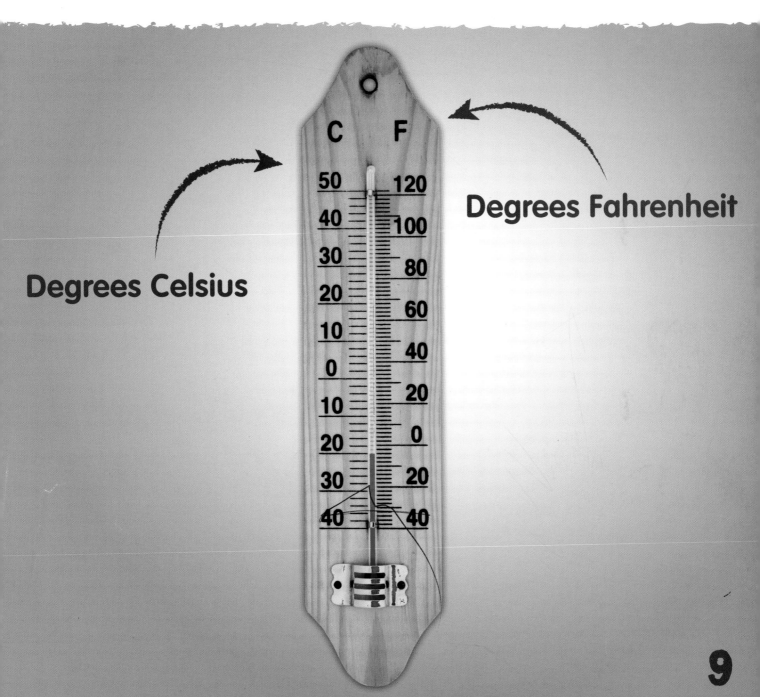

HOT
TEMPERATURES

When something has a high temperature, we say that it is hot. When people have a high temperature, it can make their bodies sweat.

We can warm up our bodies by exercising. Exercising can make us feel hot, which can also make us sweat.

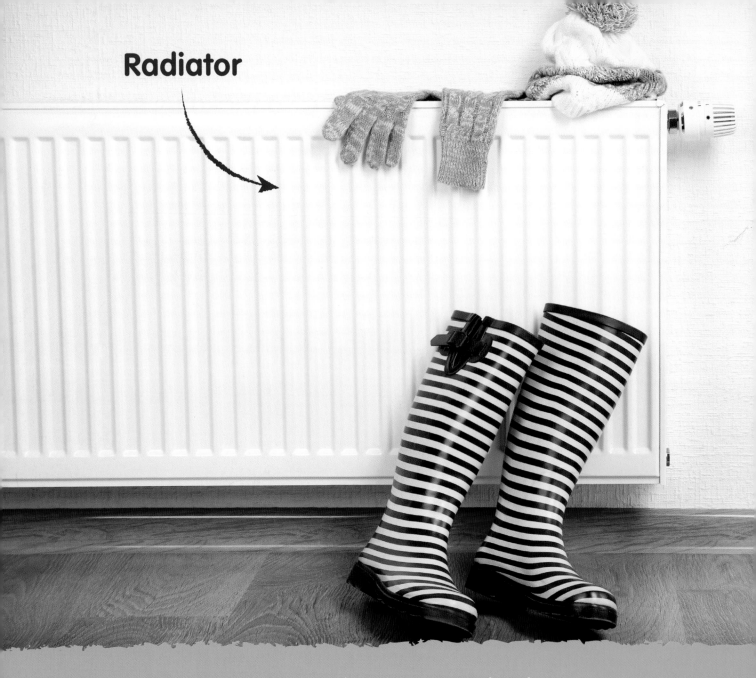

Radiator

When it is cold outside, we turn the heating on to make our houses warm. Lots of houses have radiators that give off heat.

Some people have a fireplace where they can light a fire. Fire is very hot and gives off a lot of heat.

Never stand too close to a fire. It is very hot and very dangerous.

13

HEATING
MATERIALS

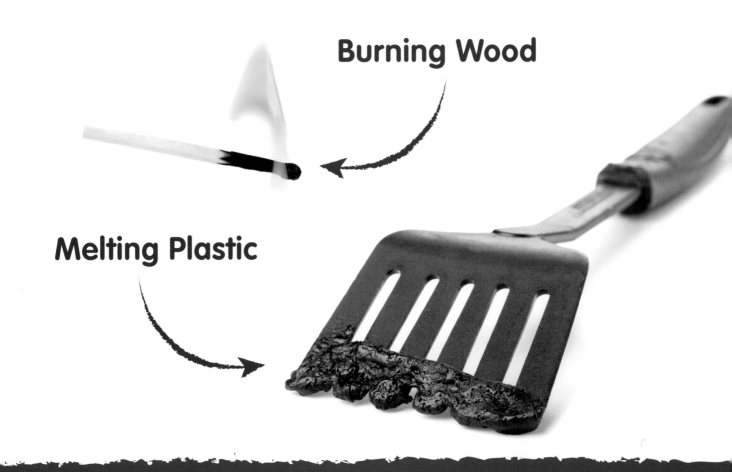

Burning Wood

Melting Plastic

Most **materials** burn or **melt** when they get very hot. Wood will burn and plastic will melt.

Even strong materials, such as metal, will melt when they are heated to a high enough temperature.

Metal

COLD
TEMPERATURES

When something has a low temperature, we say that it is cold. Ice is very cold. Sometimes we put ice in our drinks to make them colder.

We keep food and drink cold to keep it fresh.
We do this by putting it in the fridge.

Fridge

17

It often snows in winter.

When the temperature outside is very cold, it can snow.

Winter weather can make us feel cold. We keep ourselves warm by wearing thick clothes, coats and scarves.

FREEZING
MATERIALS

Some things change when they get very cold.

When water is very cold, it freezes into ice.

Water freezes at 0 degrees Celsius.

When water freezes, it changes from a **liquid** to a **solid**. Solid water is called ice.

Ice

Let's EXPERIMENT!

Do you know how to turn water into ice?
Let's find out!

STEP 1

Pour the warm water into the ice try.

STEP 2

Place the ice tray into the freezer. Be careful not to spill any of the water!

STEP 3
Leave the ice tray in the freezer for one day.

STEP 4

Remove the ice tray and push out the ice cubes.

TOP TIP:

Ask an adult
to help you!

RESULTS:

The warm water has now turned into ice!

GLOSSARY

exercising	moving your body to stay healthy
liquid	a material that flows, such as water
materials	things that objects are made out of
measure	a way to find out the size, length, amount or temperature of something
melt	to change something from a solid to a liquid
solid	stable in shape, not a liquid

INDEX